HE WOLF WAS NOT SLEEPING

AVRIL McDONALD

ILLUSTRATED BY TATIANA MININA

Crown House Publishing Limited
www.crownhouse.co.uk

Deep in the forest one
dark winter's night,
In a small cosy bed
by the fireflies' light,

A wolf lay awake.
His loud beating heart
Was thumping in fear
that the howling might start.

Tick tock went the clock,
Twit twoo called the owl,
As he prayed to the moon
that the wolves wouldn't howl.

But the forest stayed quiet
and with first morning light,
"Phew!" Wolfgang said:
everything was all right.

Each night was the same.
His loud beating heart
Would be thumping in fear
that the howling might start.

And if all was still quiet
by first morning light,
"Phew!" he would say:
everything was all right.

But this peace wouldn't last,
and that worried him so,
For when the wolves howled,
his dad had to go.

His dad was a helper.
When they called, he would run –
No matter where, when or how,
he'd be helping someone.

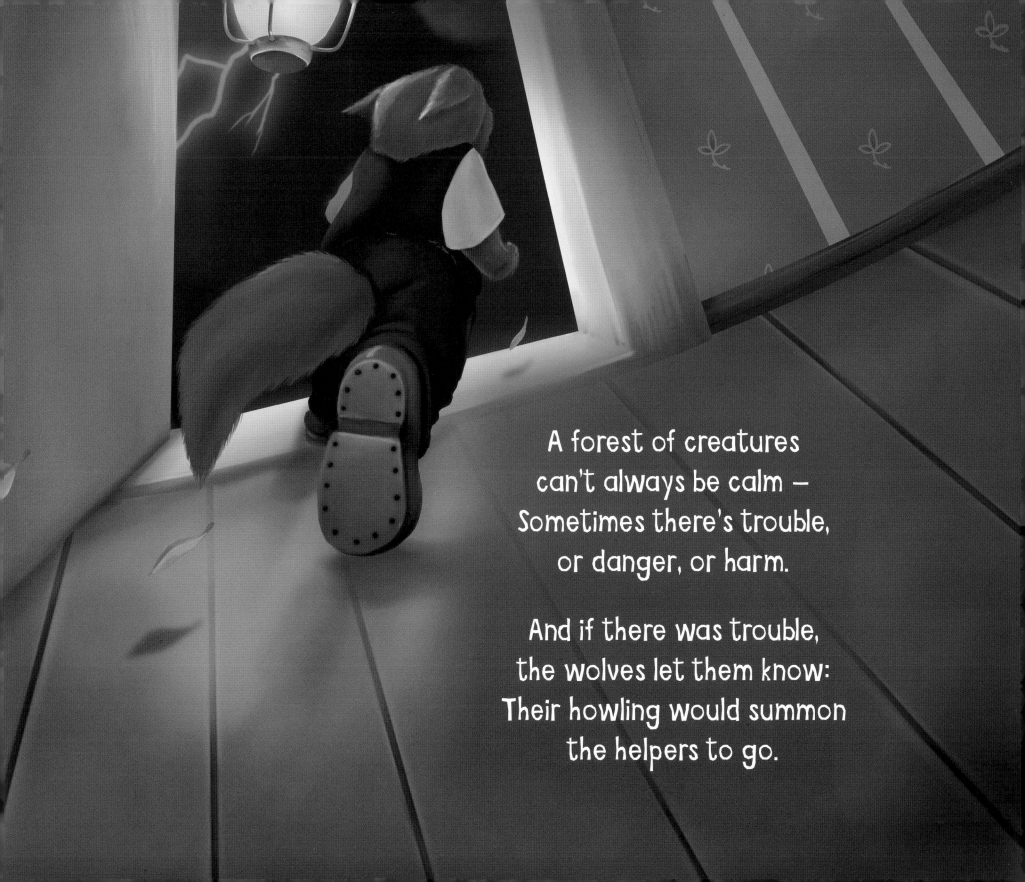

A forest of creatures
can't always be calm —
Sometimes there's trouble,
or danger, or harm.

And if there was trouble,
the wolves let them know:
Their howling would summon
the helpers to go.

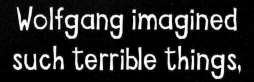

Wolfgang imagined
such terrible things,

Like dungeons and dragons
with large scaly wings,

Trolls under bridges,
villains and thieves,

Dangerous traps that
lay hidden in leaves!

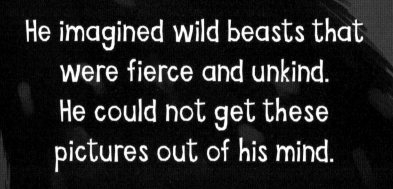

He imagined wild beasts that
were fierce and unkind.
He could not get these
pictures out of his mind.

The thought of it all
made his legs feel like jelly.
His stomach was turning
like worms in his belly.

So he lay awake worried
each night in his bed,
And was falling asleep
in the daytime instead!

Now this was a problem
when friends came to play,
For playdates most often
are during the day.

And when Wolfgang was "it"
or his turn came around,
He was fast asleep somewhere,
and not to be found!

Snoring away, he'd lie
curled in a heap,
In a game one could only call
"Hide and go sleep!"

He was struggling to think straight,
he slept during school.
When Owl asked him questions,
he felt like a fool.

Anxious and scared,
after school he would creep
Back home where he dreaded
when time came for sleep.

But tonight would be different.
He hadn't a clue
What a spider, some pens
and some magic could do.

Spider knew he
was frightened,
so did something kind.
She scribbled a note
for Big Dad Wolf to find.

We might have a problem
we think we should hide,
But a problem won't go
if it's locked up inside.

Now his dad understood,
so that night before bed,
He sat down with Wolfgang
and here's what he said:

"I know you feel scared
when the wolves start to call,
But I'm safe and you don't
have to worry at all.

I run with a team,
we're like birds of a feather!
We're a family, we're stronger
when we stick together.

There's Bisma, whose feathers
are perfectly styled.

She looks after the team
who take calls from the wild."

"Smithy's our joker

and Foxy's in charge –
She keeps cool under pressure;
we all call her 'Sarge'.

There's Ranger,
who's loyal,

Bobby

and

Slick,

And Speedy the Cat,
she's so nimble
and quick.

Then there's Hop, who is old
and incredibly kind –
He can calm creatures down
just by using his mind."

"We all run together,
we're never alone.
Each one of us makes sure
the others get home.

There are times when we're scared,
but together we're brave.
We feel pride in our hearts
for the creatures we save.

We try hard, but sometimes
a creature might die,
And this makes us feel sad,
so we talk, hug and cry."

"A lot of the time, though,
the problems are small –
Like when one does not
follow instructions at all!

The wolves when they howl
tell the world that we care,
That if anyone needs us,
they know we'll be there!

So the next time they howl
and I run to the door,
You need not be worried
like you were before."

Wolfgang just loved
that he now knew the team.
He'd learnt things aren't always
as bad as they seem.

Then he asked Big Dad Wolf,
"Now I know all the crew,
But what is the name
that the others call you?"

"It's Bear," Dad replied,
"'cause I love a big hug."
Then he gave one to Wolfgang,
who felt warm and snug.

"Good night, Dad," said Wolfgang
as he lay down his head.
"Good night, my brave wolf.
Sweet dreams," Dad Wolf said.

And now, across town,
if you look hard, you'll see
The same team – on a wall,
in a room, up a tree;

In a bedroom close by,
with trinkets galore,
And one hundred and twenty
stuffed mice to adore;

Above three little beds,
in a room with a view;

On the wall beside twins
down on Bird Avenue.

And in a small bed
by the fireflies' light,
Wolfgang sleeps soundly now,
all through the night.

And if you were to ask him
his favourite dream,
He'd say, "Running with heroes
beside Bear on the team!"